AF425229

The Death Theory

Proposed by:

Danish Rasheed

Index

"DEATH GIVES RISE TO NEW LIFE"

DANISH RASHEED

THE DEATH THEORY

Proposed: DANISH RASHEED

The universe is full of mysteries. In other words we don't know much about universe similarly we don't know much about humans. In world here are thousands of questions whose answers we don't know. Among them one of the fascinating question is "why and How living organism (human beings) die ?"

Introduction

The human body is a complex, highly organized structure made up of unique cells that work together to accomplish the specific functions necessary for sustaining life. Anatomy is organized by levels, from the smallest components of cells to the largest organs and their relationships to other organs.

A unicellular organism, also known as a single-celled organism, is an organism that consists of a single cell, unlike a multicellular organism that consists of multiple cells. ...

Biology

study of living things and their vital processes. The field deals with all the physicochemical aspects of life. The modern tendency toward cross-disciplinary research and the unification of scientific knowledge and investigation from different fields has resulted in significant overlap of the field of biology with other scientific disciplines. Modern principles of other fields—chemistry, medicine, and physics, for example—are integrated with those of biology in areas such as biochemistry, bio-medicine, and biophysics. Biology is subdivided into separate branches for convenience of study, though all the subdivisions are interrelated by basic principles. Thus, while it is custom to separate the study of plants (botany) from that of animals (zoology), and the study of the structure of organisms (morphology) from that of function (physiology), all living things share in common certain biological phenomena—for example, various means of reproduction, cell division, and the transmission of genetic material. Cell biology is the study of cells—the fundamental units of structure and function in living organisms. Cells were first observed in the 17th century, when the compound microscope was invented. Before that time, the individual organism was studied as a whole in a field known as organismic biology, that area of research remains an important component of the biological sciences. Population biology deals with groups or populations of organisms that inhabit a given area or region. Included at that level are studies of the roles that specific kinds of plants and animals play in the complex and self-perpetuating interrelationships that exist between the living and the nonliving world, as well as studies of the built-in controls that maintain those relationships naturally. Those broadly based levels—molecules, cells, whole organisms, and populations—may be further subdivided for study, giving rise to specializations such as morphology, taxonomy, biophysics, biochemistry, genetics, epigenetics, and ecology. A field of biology may be especially concerned with the investigation of one kind of living thing—for example, the study of birds in ornithology, the study of fishes in ichthyology, or the study of microorganisms in microbiology.

Unity

All living organisms, regardless of their uniqueness, have certain biological, chemical, and physical characteristics in common. All, for example, are composed of basic units known as cells and of the same chemical substances, which, when analyzed, exhibit noteworthy similarities, even in such disparate organisms as bacteria and humans. Furthermore, since the action of any organism is determined by the manner in which its cells interact and since all cells interact in much the same way, the basic functioning of all organisms is also similar.

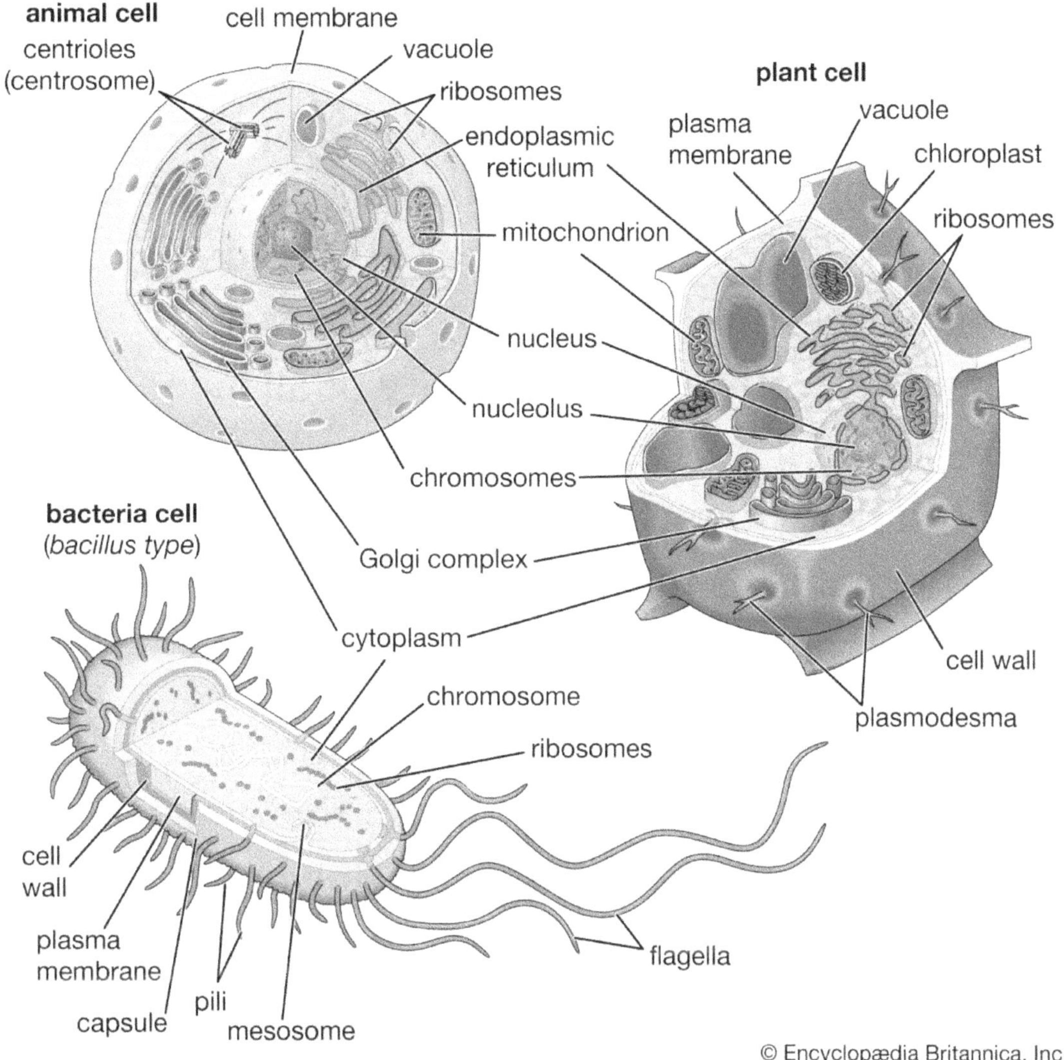

There is not only unity of basic living substance and functioning but also unity of origin of all living things. According to a theory proposed in 1855 by German pathologist Rudolf Virchow, "all living cells arise from preexisting living cells." That theory appears to be true for all living things at the present time under existing environmental conditions. If, however, life originated on Earth more than once in the past, the fact that all organisms have a sameness of basic structure, composition, and function would seem to indicate that only one original type succeeded.

A common origin of life would explain why in humans or bacteria—and in all forms of life in between—the same chemical substance, deoxyribonucleic acid (DNA), in the form of genes accounts for the ability of all living matter to replicate itself exactly and to transmit genetic information from parent to offspring. Furthermore, the mechanisms for that transmittal follow a pattern that is the same in all organisms.

Whenever a change in a gene (a mutation) occurs, there is a change of some kind in the organism that contains the gene. It is this universal phenomenon that gives rise to the differences (variations) in populations of organisms from which nature selects for survival those that are best able to cope with changing conditions in the environment.

Continuity

Whether an organism is a human or a bacterium, its ability to reproduce is one of the most important characteristics of life. Because life comes only from preexisting life, it is only through reproduction that successive generations can carry on the properties of a species.

Thanatology,

The description or study of death and dying and the psychological mechanisms of dealing with them. Thanatology is concerned with the notion of death as popularly perceived and especially with the reactions of the dying, from whom it is felt much can be learned about dealing with death's approach.

"We can't make this clam that we have 100% information about any organism in world…."

Physics...

PLANKS EQUATION...

Max Planck discovered a theory that energy is transferred in the form of chunks called as quanta, assigning as h. The variable h holds the constant value equal to 6.63 x 10-34 J.s based on International System of Units and the variable describes the frequency. The Planck's law help us calculate the energy of photons when their frequency is known.

If the wavelength is known, you can calculate the energy by using the wave equation to calculate the frequency and then apply Planck's equation to find the energy.

What is Planck's Constant?

Put differently, Plank's constant describes the relevancy between the energy per quantum (photon) of electromagnetic radiation to its frequency.

Assumption"

Living organism may differ in cell, structure, the way their body functions etc.

There are some particles or things common in every organism which supports or defines life or death and I believe (predict) among them one pair of particle which have important role in life and death have some (or may be all) characteristics like photon.

Those are...

- They have zero mass and rest **energy**.
- They are stable, have no **electric charge**.
- They carry **energy** and **momentum** which are dependent on the frequency.

Calculation

At the time of death the energy of the subject (an organism who is dying), where is it approaching, zero or infinity ?

The answer is...

$$E = h\nu \quad ; h \rightarrow \text{Planks constant}$$
$$\nu \rightarrow \text{frequency}$$
$$\text{(Max Planck's Equation)}$$

Either,

$E = 0$

Here $h \neq 0$ (planks constant)

$\Rightarrow \nu = 0$ (LINE)

Zero frequency means infinite wave length.

WAVE LENGTH...

Wave length is the spatial period of a periodic wave—the distance over which the wave's shape repeats. It is the distance between consecutive corresponding points of the same phase on the wave, such as two adjacent crests, troughs, or zero crossings, and is a characteristic of both traveling waves and standing waves, as well as other spatial wave patterns. The inverse of the wavelength is called the spatial frequency. Wavelength is commonly designated by the Greek letter *lambda* (λ). The term *wavelength* is also sometimes applied to modulated waves, and to the sinusoidal envelopes of modulated waves or waves formed by interference of several sinusoids.

Assuming a sinusoidal wave moving at a fixed wave speed, wavelength is inversely proportional to frequency of the wave. waves with higher frequencies have shorter wavelengths, and lower frequencies have longer wavelengths.

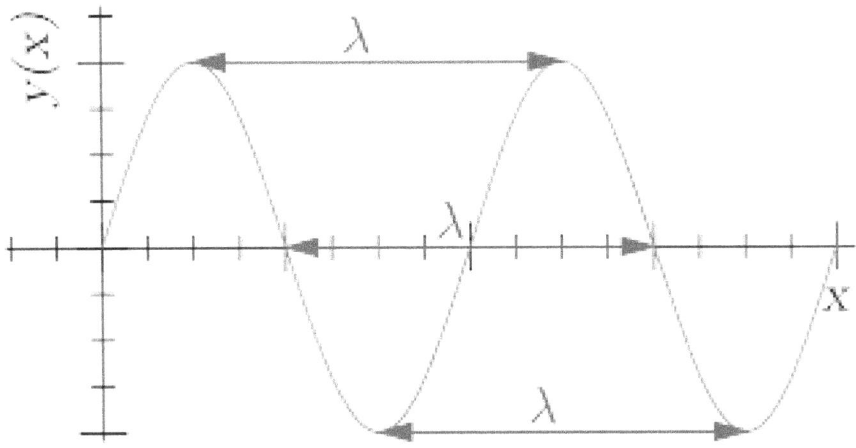

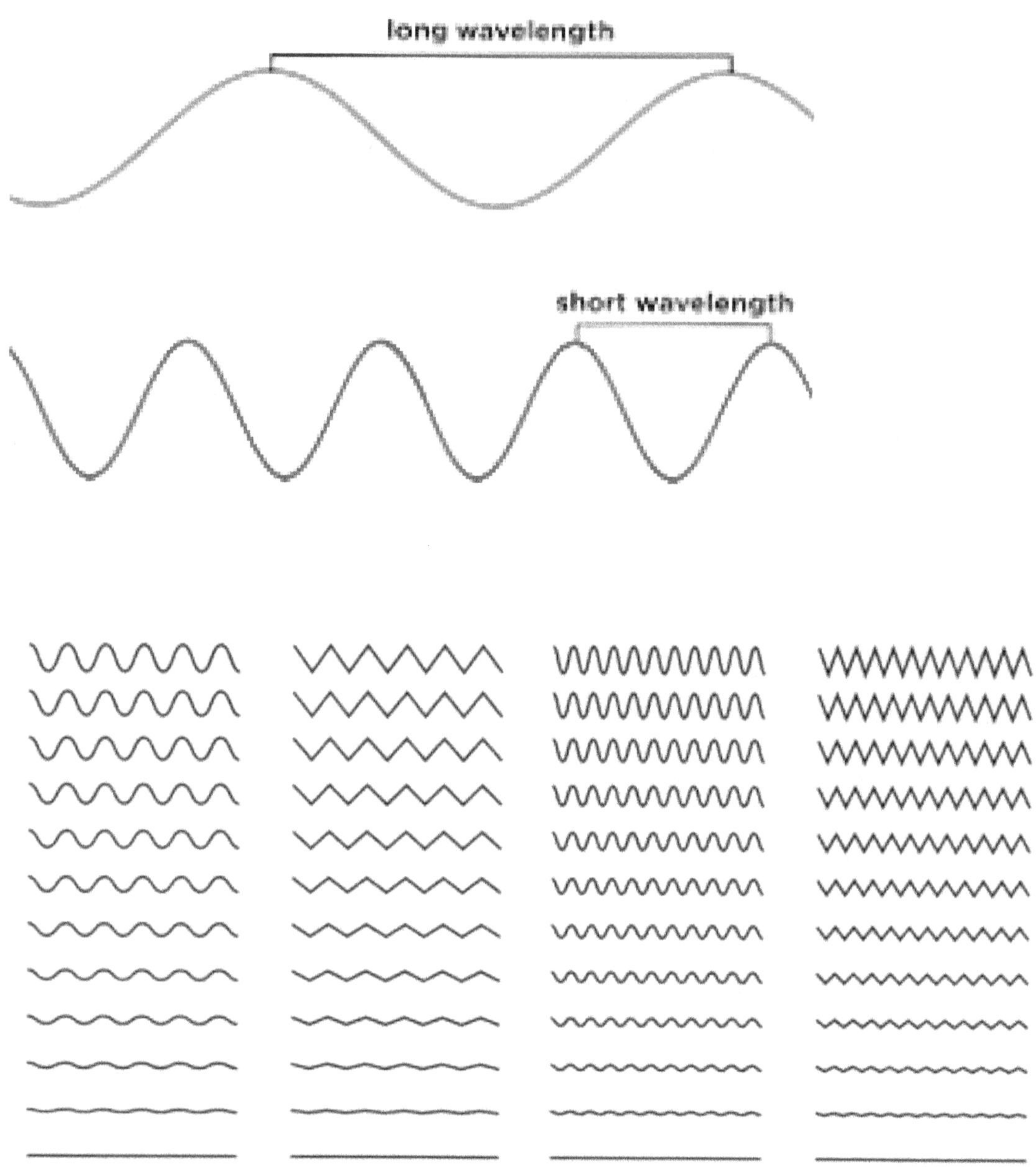

"Zero frequency is only possible *at absolute temp.*
So this case isn't possible...."
The person may be appear to be dead 24-26° C.

OR,

$E = \infty$

$$\Rightarrow v = \infty$$

I. e., $\lambda = 0$ (POINT)

Point has many definitions but I sting to " Point is line with zero length"

One more, "It is a circle with zero radius"

$\lambda = 0$,

Means the forward motion of particle seized.

Therefore, at the time of death energy approach's to infinity.

Question

How the energy of the subject approach's to infinity ?

As I already mentioned there are two types of particles like photon, lets name them "Zeton" and "Epton".

What is their work ?

Zeton carry raw energy (the energy formed by body) to unknown mechanism like factory while as Epton travels with the help of pure energy {The energy which is independent on mass (mass doesn't convert directly into pure energy) } and carry it (or utilizes it).

In body raw energy is converted into pure energy by an unknown mechanism like factory.

During dying forward motion of Epton particles seizes meanwhile Zeton keep supplying raw energy to factory (unknown mechanism) and that keeps converting raw energy into pure energy at the same rate due to which production keeps increasing and approach to infinity and subjects body doesn't tolerate such huge energy and dies {enters into new stage or fission (division)}

Why Zeton keep supplying energy ?

Because of its characteristics...

1) It has negative frequency and negative wavelength.

2) It has negative energy.

 Due to which it doesn't stop (formed motion isn't seized) and keeps functioning.

 The above calculation is for Epton.

Momentum

It product of the mass of a particle and its velocity. Momentum is a vector quantity, (it has both magnitude and direction). Isaac Newton's second law of motion states that the time rate of change of momentum is equal to the force acting on the particle.

1) What happens when Epton or Zeton like particles strike (collision) with such huge speed mass particles like cell ?

2) Are they damaging any particle ?

 When their collision happen with particles, momentum of both remains same (elastic collision) To understand this,

<u>Elastic collision;</u>

Consider in body collision happen between a cell (with mass m) has velocity V after collision U and Epton (with m=0) particle has velocity v in body. Therefore, by elastic collision formula,

$mV + 0(v) = mu + 0(u)$

$\Rightarrow mV = mu$

Which states, momentum (or velocity) of mass particle remains unaffected.

Due to their collision with mass particle remains undamaged because in destructive collision both collision objects (particles) should have mass.

Embryology
Embryology is the branch of biology that studies the prenatal development of gametes (sex cells), fertilization, and development of embryos and fetuses. Additionally, embryology encompasses the study of congenital disorders that occur before birth, known as teratology.

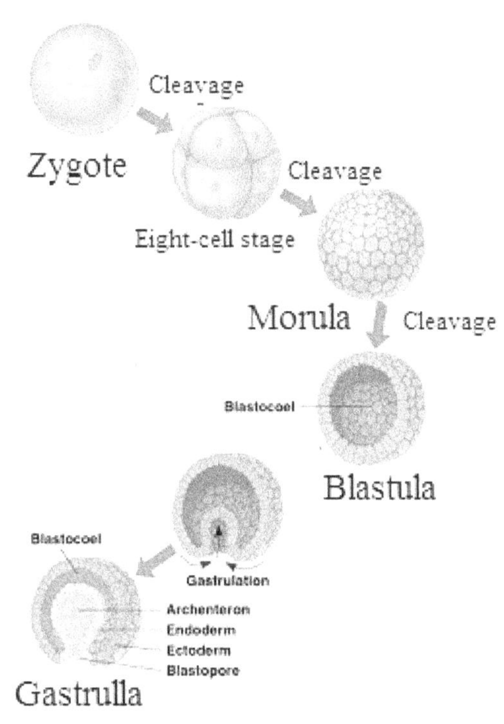

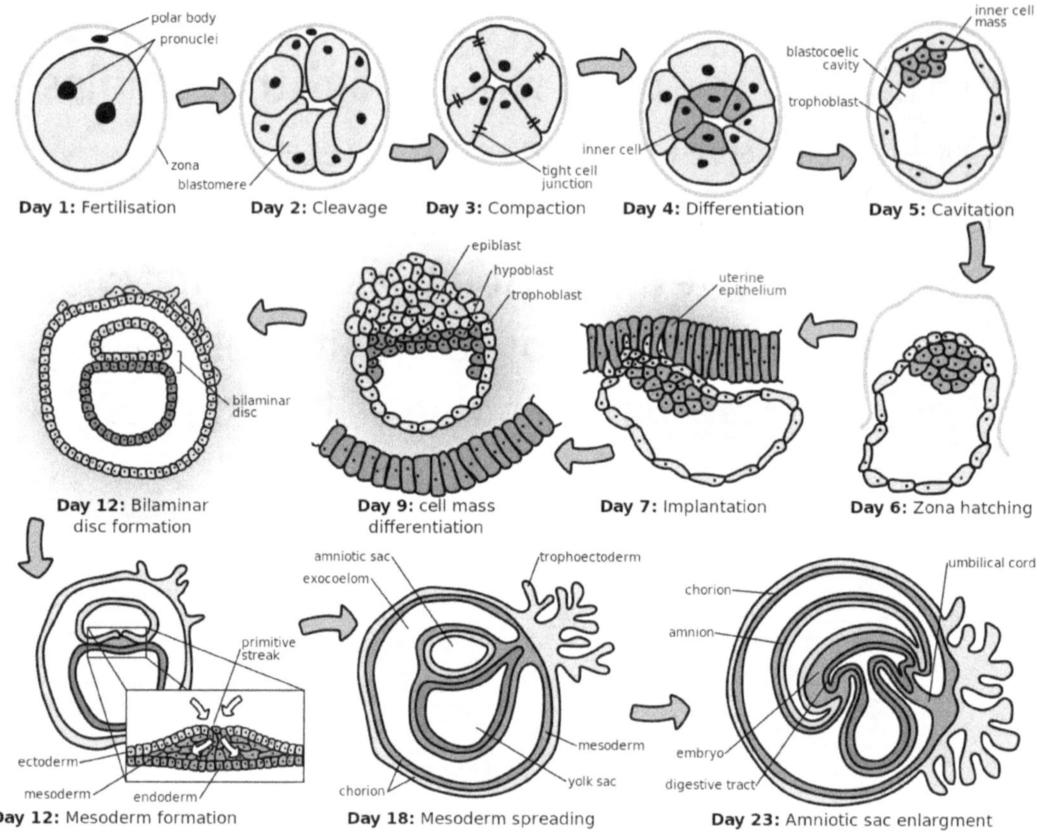

Death

Lets have a look on embryology,

When sperm fuses (life) with ovum/egg (life) result comes zygote (life), life merges with life and gives life. In other words death of sperm and egg gives rise to Zygote. Zygote leads, Morula to Blastula to Blastocyst. Every time you realize the rise of new system means like death of previous system.

While as in unicellular organisms, they undergo fission either binary or multiple.

Therefore,

"Death is a process which transfers organism from one stage of life to another."

Math...,

Probability

Probability is the branch of mathematics concerning numerical descriptions of how likely an event (event can be defined as a set of outcomes of an experiment. In other words, an event in probability is the subset of the respective sample space) is to occur, or how likely it is that a proposition is true. The probability of an event is a number between 0 and 1, where, roughly speaking, 0 indicates impossibility of the event and 1 indicates certainty.

Set,

An organized collection of objects and can be represented in set-builder form or roster form. Usually, sets are represented in curly braces {}. Set is usually represented by the capital letter. The elements that are written in the set can be in any order but cannot be repeated and separated by comma.

Limits,

A limit is defined as a number approached by the function as an independent function's variable approaches a particular value. For instance, for a function f(x) = 4x, you can say that "The limit of f(x) as x approaches 2 is 8". Symbolically, it is written as;

$\lim_{x\to 2}(4x) = 4\times 2 = 8$

 A limit is defined as a number approached by the function as an independent function's variable approaches a particular value. For instance, for a function f(x) = 5x, you can say that "The limit of f(x) as x approaches 2 is 10". Symbolically, it is written as;

$\lim_{x\to 2}(5x) = 5\times 2 = 10.$

*) $\lim_{n\to\infty} n/n + 1 = 1$

Probability of life,
Let X;E be an organism (alive) with "X" number of cells and with energy E.
After its death,
$nX;E_y$ be an organism (after the death of alive one) with energy E.
Therefore life set (L) is,
$L = (X;E, nX;E_y)$
The probability of new life with the characteristic as old life is,

$$P(L_n) = \frac{nX;E_y}{n+1}$$

$$= \frac{n}{n+1} X; E_{y'} \qquad ...(1)$$

When n approach to infinity then,
$P(L_n) = X;E_{y'}$
Means *life came back with new energy.*

Where it happens,
In the unicellular organisms,
   In ...(1), if n = 1 then,
$P(L_n) = 0.5X; E_{y'}$
Means daughter cell is the half of the parent cell with energy $E_{y'}$
Fission leads always parent cell to even count of daughter cell.
Fission happens always along line of symmetry (in both binary and multiple).
Note: For your understanding you can replace X by 1.

What about multicellular organisms ?

Probability (Multi-cellular)

X;E be an organism (alive) with "X" number of cells and with energy E.
After its death,
Its cell count circa remains same which implies,
New life as characteristics as old be X;E
Therefore, life set (L) is,
L = (X;E)
$P(L_n) = P(Lo) = X;E$
But as we know in old life energy is rising to infinity therefore it has to enter into new stage of life.

Another Method

X;E be an organism (alive) with "X" number of cells and with energy E.

After its death,

$nX;E_y$ be an organism (after the death of alive one) with energy E.

Therefore life set (L) is,

$L = (X;E)$

The probability of new life with the characteristic as old life is,

$$P(L_n) = \underline{X;E_y}$$

$$= X; E_{y'}$$

The factor of new life is same as that of old. And results is again (as in first method),

Energy is infinity so life will enter into new stage.

What is after here ?

I don't know but I am cent percent sure after here we will be more complex and advance.

Conclusion

1) When in a body of an organism energy approach to in infinity, death happens.

2) Death is a process which transfers living organisms from stage to another.

Death gives rise to new life.

3) Death leads you to new stage or fission depends what you are(multicellular or uni-cellular).

4) Death happens in fraction of time (As v approach to infinity, time approach to zero)

Life is conserved, it is because of energy.

About author

Myself Danish Rasheed from Dooru Shahabad (192211). I'm a student of aerospace engineering, studying in HITS Chennai (603103).

I tried to explain as simple as I could, if you have any doubt anywhere in this booklet then you can contact me on,

sage_hemu_jee

danishrasheedofficial

Sage Hemu jee

Notes of Source

Biology, unity,continuity, Thanatology, Planks Equation, Wave length, Embryology, Probability set and limits have source of internet in order to you understand clearly the required concept.

Assumption, Calculation, Question, Death, Probability of life (multi-cellular) and conclusion are my (Danish Rasheed) thoughts.

Thanks for reading...

Notes